UNITY AND TRUTH
IN THE
CHURCH OF ENGLAND

UNITY AND TRUTH
IN THE
CHURCH OF ENGLAND

by

J. F. BETHUNE-BAKER, D.D.

*Lady Margaret's Professor of Divinity
in the University of Cambridge*

CAMBRIDGE
AT THE UNIVERSITY PRESS
1934

CAMBRIDGE
UNIVERSITY PRESS

University Printing House, Cambridge CB2 8BS, United Kingdom

Cambridge University Press is part of the University of Cambridge.

It furthers the University's mission by disseminating knowledge in the pursuit of education, learning and research at the highest international levels of excellence.

www.cambridge.org
Information on this title: www.cambridge.org/9781107505759

© Cambridge University Press 1934

First published 1934

A catalogue record for this publication is available from the British Library

ISBN 978-1-107-50575-9 Paperback

I

"That they all may be one." Jn xvii, 21.[1]

In the great prayer which has this as its chief petition a distinction is drawn between "the world" and the men and women in it who, in any age, are brought to see in Jesus the manifestation of the one true GOD of all the world—His name, His characteristics (*v.* 6, ἐφανέρωσά σου τὸ ὄνομα). It is an ideal for Christians among themselves "that they all may be one"—"even as thou, Father, art in me, and I in thee, that they also may be in us...that they may be one, even as we are one".

That the prayer as we have it is the evangelist's own composition is clear, but that it is a true reflexion of the mind of Jesus on this point we cannot doubt. It is worth noting that by the time the prayer was recorded there was need to proclaim the ideal as persuasively as possible: the evangelist had in view a need of the young society. The wonder of the new experience of which Jesus was the centre had already found different kinds of expression. Different descriptions

[1] A sermon preached in St Andrew's, Ashley Place, at the Annual Meeting of the Modern Churchman's Union on Wednesday, May 30, 1934.

of it which could crystallize into historical facts and theological definitions were current. Good practices with religious intention were becoming conventions or sacred institutions. Convenient arrangements for the decent order of affairs in the various groups of believers were having the authority of apostles or of the Lord Himself claimed for them. Already there were many groups; ecclesiastical organizations and systems of doctrine were in the making.

As for doctrine, in the very act of writing his Gospel the evangelist was himself putting out a new interpretation of the significance of Jesus. The oneness which he thought was in accordance with his Master's mind clearly allowed of various ways of conceiving Him: it did not demand one only formulation—a single creed. And as to organization, in the allegory of the Good Shepherd, which deals in story form with the same conception of unity, it is not one fold but one flock that the one shepherd wants. Those that are his, given to him by the Father, may be distributed in many folds on earth—yea, even in heaven, in the Father's house "there are many mansions" waiting to receive them—while yet they all may be one.

We know, indeed, that Jerome by his change of *una grex* to *unum ovile* in the Latin version which became the Bible of the Western Church, and Augustine by his use of the mistranslation in his conflict with some early puritan schismatics, have a heavy responsibility for the "one-fold" theory that prevailed in the West. But already before their time uniformity of creed, with technical definitions that only specialists can understand, had come, and uniformity of order was already regarded as the divinely appointed channel through which alone a true religion here and eternal life hereafter could be obtained.

As we look back on those far-off times, the early years and on through the middle ages, it may well seem to us that only so in all the changing conditions of the world of those days—only so could Christianity have survived and kept such kind of identity as it undoubtedly has preserved. At all events it was the "one-fold" theory that gave us the continuity we have, both outward and visible and inward and spiritual. It gave us, first, as our criterion of the Christian faith the New Testament—that great treasury of different points of view from which we can always quote some text wherewith to confound our opponents, till they quote another for us to be confounded in turn. It gave us our glorious heritage of Christian literature in which, in every age, I suppose, we can find something that makes us feel our spiritual kinship. However far forward we have moved today, whatever ideas of the past we have discarded with growing knowledge of the world that is for the moment our world and has always been God's world —of all the pain and travail and adventure of which we are the outcome—yet as we read the Christian literature of almost any previous age, bizarre and strange and uncongenial as so much of it is, we feel that we are in the same religious tradition, lawful heirs and trustees of it.

To get to know thee, the only true God, and Jesus Christ whom thou didst send.

Other foundation can no man lay than that which is laid, which is Jesus Christ.

...who loved me and gave himself for me.

To be carnally minded is death, but to be spiritually minded is life and peace.

Thou, O God, didst make us for thyself, and the heart of man is restless till it finds rest in thee.

> Rock of ages, cleft for me,
> Let me hide myself in thee.

These are notes that are re-echoed all down the ages, and where they are silent we miss a characteristic unitive Christian experience. It is not mere sentimental emotion but the fine flower of mind and heart in personal expression.

When we pass beyond description like this to

reasoned doctrines and definitions, of course we come to what is not unitive but divisive.

The results of the one-fold theory in the formulation of order and explanation have been the disruptions and disunions that have set Christian so-called against Christian all the world over. And it is because this same theory seems still to possess the official mind of the Churches of Rome and of England that recent conversations and discussions about re-union are watched by the rank and file of all the English communions concerned with indifference or disdain and resentment. The kind of re-union that seems to be in view is based on a false conception of unity. It is the ecclesiastical mind that must be converted, if the mind of Christ is ever to rule in the churches of Christendom. How the call of the Christ comes to us to-day—μετανοεῖτε all ye Christian ecclesiastics, clerical and lay alike. Get a new point of view. Must ye for ever, in these matters, be tithing mint and anise and cummin?

I suppose we should want to answer, But O Master! Master of the things of the spirit, the abiding things of worth, must we not still pay heed to these things, for we are still on the plane of this world? Is it not true, "On earth the broken arc, In heaven the perfect round"? In Thine own little band of twelve was there not organization, an inner circle of three (Peter and James and John, who all had ideas of their own), and one with a money-bag, the business man of the band who wanted to make a public success of Thy cause? Surely it *need not* have been just he who betrayed Thee? Must ecclesiastical statesmanship always involve betrayal?

We cannot help it. Creeds and institutions we must have, and systems of doctrine to answer, however lamely, the questions of that spirit within us by which alone we are human but which we believe is also the "candle of the Lord". Only when it is well trained and instructed can we avoid "profane and idle babblings" in our discourse of high things. We know it is "in his heart" that the Christian must "sanctify Christ as Lord", but he is also bidden to be ready always to give a reasoned account concerning the hope that is in him (I Pet. iii, 15). I do not think he can do this to-day, any more than he could seven or seventeen centuries ago, by a selection of bits of description from the New Testament. Something more reasoned than that seems to me to be required in our present environment of thought and knowledge and our search for a coherent conception of human experience as it is spread out before us to-day.

For my own part, at least in the statement of my creed, I cannot let go the great findings of the past in the doctrines of the Incarnation and the Trinity. I do not mean the popular conceptions of them in terms of a sudden miraculous intrusion from outside or of three individual centres of consciousness. These conceptions I suppose we all regard as modes of valuation that are out of date, or examples of the high mythology dependent on human analogies with which Religion gives, as it were, flesh and blood to its otherwise dumb convictions. And we should add that, in so doing, in the case of these doctrines it testifies to the fact that they are based on actual happenings on this homely earth of ours and the actual experience of men and women like ourselves.

But the fundamental idea of Incarnation, as it can be presented to-day in the light of our view of evolutionary, epigenetic, process, and the idea of the Trinity as our Christian philosophers have portrayed it, seem to me to define the lines along which we reach the true interpretation of human life and history. We may recognize some kind of Christian sentiment and aspiration, some kind of Christian direction of life, where these ideas are wanting. But if there be a theology that excludes them, or even ignores them as indifferent, I at least cannot deem it a "Christian" theology or believe that it could in itself suggest the Christian conception of man and the world and God, and so direct us to that fulfilment of ourselves in all

our relations with one another that our old theologies
call the redemption of ourselves and the world.

> ...flesh that I seek
> In the Godhead. I seek and I find it.

> nor soul helps flesh
> More now, than flesh helps soul.

That the human is the organ of the divine; that the
flesh, the material, is the means of expression of the
soul, the spiritual; that the eternal is realized in and
through the temporal, the one only in the many and
the many only in the one, unity in diversity and
diversity in unity—these ideas, of which our doctrines
of the Incarnation and the Trinity are the classical
expression, are achievements of the human spirit in
vital connexion with early Christian experience that
has been continuous to this moment. They must, I
think, remain as the very core of our Christian Creed.
It is failure to uphold them that has led to the "profane babblings" and the -isms of the past and the
present.

Yet surely we ought to have learnt by now that of
all the detailed schemes of doctrine, as of all the forms
of order, that have been devised no one can be binding
on all Christians. In our own Church of England
we have gone farther than this. We know that even
within a particular fold, a particular Church, variant
conceptions of its institutions and widely different

interpretations of its formularies and doctrines have existed and can exist. Ever since the Reformation—that age of spiritual giants and watchful statesmen—it has been so. To keep us both Catholic and Protestant was the aim of our sixteenth-century divines. Our new Catholics of to-day dislike the word Protestant, but I do not believe that their leaders really have a narrower aim. In any case, as far as we can discern the genius of the Church of England and the religious tradition of the English people, it will never be confined in any narrower conception of ecclesiastical order and institutions than our Reformation settlement reflects. Rather it will seek a still wider catholicity to embrace its world-wide dispersion and the many other races whose special contribution to the interpretation of the Gospel it seems to be its destiny to welcome and honour with its own.

The new revelation of knowledge, of the world and the Bible and the beginnings of the Christian religion, has already spread its light among ourselves. The older ones of us here could point to landmarks and crises in its course of not much more than seventy years. I recall to-day one of the last of these crises, just twenty years ago. The new number of *Theology* which came to me yesterday reminds me of it. A great leader of the Church flung down a grave, if somewhat petulant, challenge to the methods of study pursued to-day wherever Truth is the aim. There was much talk about the "historical facts of the Creed", the "literal" and the "legal" construction of its clauses, and a mixture of literal and symbolical interpretation. A new phrase appeared, the "religious construction", which could be applied to all clauses alike; and it was claimed that in such religious construction only could continuity of Christian faith be found and maintained. To-day, as far as my own experience goes, it is only in such religious construction of our Creeds that educated men and women have any interest.

So in these great matters of the re-interpretation of ancient creeds, of free historical and scientific enquiry, and of refusal to be tied by old beliefs, our fold has shewn itself to be one with expanding walls. And it is the peculiar concern of "modern" Churchmen, of all generations and of all schools, to see to it that the walls never close in on them in these respects. They will do so always, of course, with the "sweet reasonableness" which is the mark of Christian strength and the "meekness and godly fear" of a good conscience. I suppose that means with courtesy because they are sure of their ground, keeping their tempers, even when their opponents "furiously rage together" and "imagine a vain thing". And they will do so in full confidence that, however far short they fall in other respects, in this they are true to their Master's ideal—

true to the ideal of the one-ness of the flock for which he prayed.

In the world as it is, with its rich varieties of types of human personality and ways and means of expression, there may well continue particular modes of presenting the common Christian conviction, our Christian Faith. Particular folds may remain. And to-day there are many who are not in any fold whom yet, it may be, the Shepherd of the flock knows as His own. For somehow they hear His voice and know Him as their leader; in heart, if not in mind, they recognize in Him the manifestation of the one true God and the way of life for mankind. And the heart, which has its own reasons, guides them to find no narrower fold than the human society to which we all belong. In it, in service to their neighbour, they set forth the ideals of Christ and in their own way worship His God. Between them and Christians who can be labelled there is a real unity of spirit, and perhaps we must be content with that. But if between others who stand in conscious relation to the same Master ecclesiastical statesmanship cannot find the way to visible inter-communion, it must be because it is distracted by irrelevant interests and aims, and has not learnt, even yet, the meaning of the prayer "that they all may be one".

II

"But ye did not so learn Christ; if so be that ye heard him, and were taught in him, even as truth is in Jesus." Eph. iv, 20, 21.[1]

"Even as truth is in Jesus." These are very remarkable words. I have no scruple in asking for your earnest attention to them this afternoon, however unworthy of the theme my treatment of it must be.

And I do not hesitate to assume, as I should be entitled to assume in any church in Christendom, that for everyone joining in our Christian worship the truth as truth is in Jesus is no mere question of abstract speculation but one of vital concern. Nay, more, I shall venture to assume that, among all the goodly pearls of truth of many kinds which a man might rightly spend his life in seeking, this truth, as truth is in Jesus, if only he could find it, would be the one pearl of great price which he might with good reason go and sell all that he had to buy (Mt. xiii, 45).

For it is our religion at its core that is concerned. What the writer of this Epistle has in mind is not just the teaching of Jesus.

In the long and wonderful history of man's adventurous and painful course in the world great

---

[1] A sermon preached in Westminster Abbey on Sunday, June 10, 1934.

teachers have emerged and taught to others what it was given to them to see and to learn. The followers of such great teachers have desired to understand their Master's teaching, and almost always they have disputed about it and broken up into schools, some seizing on one element in the teaching, some on another, and making it by itself the heart of a system. Many of us to-day who are conscious of what we owe in the make-up of our minds to great thinkers of the past might call ourselves Platonists, Wordsworthians, Darwinians, because we believe that some of the ideas of the great philosopher, poet, man of science were true, and have helped to make us what we are. But it would never occur to us to speak of truth as truth is in a Plato, a Wordsworth, a Darwin. We know them only through their teaching, their writings.

Jesus, our Lord, as a teacher, was in the line of the great prophets of his race whose writings remain for us among our sacred books; but, as every one knows, we have no writings from him. Once only is he recorded to have written and then it was on sand—and no one knows what it was that he wrote.

And even his teaching has only come to us in fragments. There are hardly any quotations of his actual words in the earlier parts of our New Testament. No doubt we have enough in the Gospels which were written later to make us feel that we do know a good deal about what he taught; yet it is all dependent on recollection after many years and translation from Aramaic into Greek. If we could attribute to him the deliberate intention which is freely invoked by apologists of some institutions of the Church that are clearly of later growth, we should say that he deliberately avoided the risk that any of his followers should have words of his out of which to make a system of rules or a Creed. He trusted to something less formal, at once more free and elusive and much more pervasive, a "spirit".

All that he ever actually taught his disciples by rote, so to say, was not a Creed, but a prayer: they had asked him, Lord teach us to pray: they wanted a formula; and he taught them "the Lord's Prayer". But even that they either could not remember exactly or could not leave alone: for it comes to us in different forms.

So it certainly is not the teaching of Jesus that is meant by truth as truth is in Jesus. It is the kind of greater thing to which he himself alluded when he referred to the old story of the Queen of Sheba and said she "came from the ends of the earth to hear the wisdom of Solomon, and lo, more than Solomon is here"; or again "a greater thing than the temple is here" (Mt. xii, 42; Luke xi, 31; Mt. xii, 6).

Indeed this truth as truth is in Jesus, as Christians came to conceive it, is something that could not have been conceived in his lifetime. It was not yet there to be conceived. It needed the Death on the Cross and the experience—his own and his disciples'—that followed, before that truth could emerge in the evolutionary process of the world, the natural historical process, which is, as we believe, the way of the Divine education of mankind. So it was at once a human achievement and discovery and a new revelation of the Divine activity of the Creator and Preserver of the world: a new event.

And so we all know that we have in this event, this fact of Jesus, a landmark in the history of the world.— But this event, this fact of Jesus, is not simply Jesus himself; and truth as truth is in Jesus is not simply truth about Jesus. It is the true appreciation, or valuation, of the whole experience which had its centre in him—this early Christian experience which is not so much recorded as reflected in our New Testament.

No one, whether Christian or not, who reads its pages to-day, after all these years, can fail to perceive that he is confronted by an unparalleled human experience. He will feel of course that it is all set in a framework of human culture and science and mentality from which later progress of civilization and knowledge and economic order has passed away. He must of course read it and see it in its framework. But, if he is to get at the experience itself, just that which is really revealing in it, he must be prepared to eliminate as irrelevant all in the record that belongs merely to the science of the period. It is true that Christians in general have hardly yet learnt to see all these things in a true perspective. But no intelligent reader can fail to notice that of the wonder which it reflects our New Testament gives us different descriptions and shews that it was approached in those early days from different angles and points of view. The New Testament contains no doubt a good deal of history, but all of it is of the nature of valuation. Other stories, other points of view, other valuations were current among Christians, some of which are still known to students of the beginnings of our religion. But when the Church in the second century collected together those that we all know, and so made up as it were one volume of Christian Scriptures—when the Church so made and gave us as a possession for ever the New Testament—what it did was to rule out all other competing accounts and descriptions and sanction those only that the New Testament contains. It was the Church's own act, the Church's own judgement long after the events, the Church's own valuation.

Some of those early Christians were quite as intelligent as we are to-day even though they did not know all that we know to-day. They knew that different writers approached the subject from different points of view, but they put them all on a par together.

To-day perhaps we are more conscious than they were of the fact that, when anything new in your experience occurs to you, you can give no account of it except in terms of what you already know, and your old ideas get mixed up with the new ones. And the ideas and knowledge you already have may be but a poor medium for the expression of an experience that is spiritual, religious. Often it is the gifted painter who has the best medium at his command, or the story-teller skilled in making pictures out of words, or the great poet who can create for us "the light that never was on sea or land".

So it is that in our New Testament we have several kinds of valuation of the new experience of which Jesus was the centre. Let me take three of these; first one by St Paul. This Pauline valuation is based on the idea of the Messiah who was to come to restore the kingdom to Israel, and it is woven through and through with the ideas of the Jewish schools of theology which have little or no meaning for us to-day. But the idea of the Messiah is immeasurably enriched and expanded to embrace the new conception of Jesus as the Son of God "who loved me and gave himself for me", who "was rich and became poor", who regarded his high estate as his not for self-aggrandisement but as a means of service and poured himself out for the good of mankind, even to death on the cross—a Christ who could live in you, and you in him.

Then there is one by St John. This "Johannine" valuation accepts the ideas of the Christ and the Son of God, but is based on an entirely different idea—the thought of the *Logos* of God—His reason, purpose, will, mind, spirit, Word—the term includes so much—the *Logos* of God, from the very beginning immanent in the world as the life of all that is and the light that enlightens every man, at last becoming visible in human form as Man: the Logos became flesh. Jesus is the Logos. And so from this point of view, this philosophical approach, we get the doctrine of the Incarnation.

Or again from the story-teller's and the poet's approach we have the narratives of the wonderful birth and the wise men from the East, shot through and through with poetic imagination.

There was the new fact of Jesus, a man living among men in this world of ours. But he seemed to belong to another world. Nature had not produced

him. It was another world he came from. Not from
this homely earth, but from

> yonder, worlds away,
> Where the strange and new have birth
> And Power comes full in play

—a world of pilot stars and dreams and visions and
angels' songs. How else could these things be?

This particular valuation is really the least signifi-
cant of all. What does it matter how Jesus was born?
What matters is what he was, what people found in
him, so that they came to see in him in his whole
human life on earth a revelation of the divine—
Saviour and Lord—before ever any such story of
his birth was told. But these stories give us the
same valuation expressed in a way that everyone
could understand more easily than they could
the other ways of expression. Valuation and
fact were merged in one, and belief that these
stories give us plain and simple history has been
regarded as identical with belief in the doctrine of
the Incarnation.

In its scheme of doctrine the Church has blended
all these ideas together, and many others that it took
over later on from the philosophy of the time in
which some of its leaders had been trained. It built
them all up into an imposing system with careful
definitions designed to exclude all theories that

seemed to conflict, in one way or another, with its early faith.

The history of Catholic Doctrine is full of the record of such heresies and -isms, with nice discriminations that only trained theologians can appreciate aright.

These nice discriminations served their purpose at the time and (for my own part) I do not think that the Church of Christ in its presentation of truth as truth is in Jesus can ever dispense with the great ideas represented by its doctrines of the Incarnation and the Trinity. But those ideas themselves may be presented to-day in other forms and ways. We are not tied down to old ways of thought and expression.

At the great awakening—intellectual and spiritual —of five and six centuries ago the "one-fold" theory of the Church broke down irreparably; and the further enlightenment that has come since then in our outlook on the past history of the world and man has put the "one creed" theory in the same position—the theory, that is, that Christians are pledged for ever to definitions of their Faith in terms of an obsolete philosophy and science.

The heresies and -isms that were condemned in the past are simply not relevant to Christian thought to-day. No one holds them—they are out of relation to the environment of our time. The old labels do not describe what anyone thinks to-day. What particular fold you belong to, what particular label you bear, is largely accidental, the result of old conflicts and old associations:—you stay in the fold in which you were born. There are differences of ethos—here more stress than there on points of order, or on sacraments, or on details of doctrine. You are more at ease in your own fold than you would be in any other, as people often are in their own home and their own circle of friends. But all are one in the main valuation of the past—the great ideas for which the doctrines of the Incarnation and the Trinity stand.

Even the name Unitarian, that seems in word to deny this main valuation, does not tell you how those who bear that label to-day would describe their conception of truth as truth is in Jesus. For to-day in the present state of thought and knowledge their conception of GOD and Man and the World may be as Christian as any one's. For let me, please, say again —Truth as truth is in Jesus is not only truth about Jesus—a doctrine about Him. It is, for Christians, truth about the whole mystery of life, about GOD and Man and the World. Above all else, I think, it is truth about ourselves.

It is truth about ourselves that we believe was given to us and discovered in the personality and life of Jesus:—a truth we can grasp with our minds and

hearts alike, and so live out in our lives. In thinking
of Jesus as pre-eminently the Son of God, one with
God in mind and purpose and will—in all, that is to
say, that makes up what we call our "being"—living
and dying for the salvation of the world, we have set
forth to us, as in no other way, the conception of
Love as the very heart of the universe, the spring of all
life that is really life, and so the key to the meaning
of all our experience here.

The doctrine of the Incarnation is a doctrine about
ourselves. It commends the love of God for us and
to us as no other doctrine does. It shews us the real
worth and values of our own lives and for our own
lives.

The Church of Christ exists to proclaim for ever
to mankind this truth about themselves. Everything
else in the many systems of organized religion is only
of value as the channel or means by which this truth
can be vitalized in us.

Wherever, then, we find this truth as the ground
of a man's life, we ought to disregard all labels of this
or that -ism with which he is accidentally connected
and recognize in him one who, by whatever means
and ways, has learnt the truth as truth is in Jesus and
has found the pearl of great price.

And it ought to be easy for us of the Church of
England to do this, because in our own particular fold

all the differences of ethos to which I have referred on points of order and institutions such as episcopacy and sacraments, on the true relation between Church and State, on the interpretation of our traditional scheme of doctrine are represented and allowed among us. Were there time now I could give instances within my own life-time of more and more freedom in all these matters won within the Church of England as established in this realm:—more particularly freedom to use old definitions and formularies not in their literal or legal sense, but according to their religious construction. A particular theory about these things may seem to be dominant at a particular moment, but never yet to the exclusion of other theories. About these things we are not united. We are united in the use of our constitution with all the individual freedom of thought and speech that is our national possession. We are united because we have one common aim—to get to know what truth as truth is in Jesus really is for us, generation after generation, with the one common conviction, that if we know that, we know the way to the life eternal, here and now, and have the chance of living it, whatever may be hereafter. We are going in the right direction.

III

As the facts of recent history in the Church of England that bear on the subject of these sermons are not as widely known as they might be, and are often conveniently ignored in some quarters in which they are known, as though they were things to be ashamed of, it seems worth while to recall some of them here.

1. Twenty years ago, in 1914, for some months before the Great War, we had before us the questions which are raised again in the current number of *Theology* (June, 1934). It had been claimed that belief in the Incarnation and the Resurrection did not depend on belief in the stories of the Birth of Jesus and the Empty Tomb, and that clergymen who did not believe in those stories might nevertheless recite the clauses of the Apostles' Creed and profess their faith in its terms because their intention was to affirm the same religious conviction and to make their own the same theological valuation which was expressed of old in the words of the Creed.

The result of a careful and memorable debate in the House of Bishops was to leave such clergymen with their full rights of ministry in the Church of their fathers. Though the Bishops themselves reaffirmed their belief in "the historical facts" of the Creeds, they did not take action to silence such clergymen or exclude them from office in the Church. It was one of their own body, who had desired that such action should be taken, who withdrew soon afterwards from the exercise of his office as a diocesan bishop to devote himself to writing as the means of propagating his views.

It remains therefore that the ministry of the Church of England is open to men who believe in the Incarnation and the Resurrection and use the Creeds according to the religious construction of their clauses though they cannot affirm them, clause by clause, in their literal meaning.

When the question was raised again in Convocation in 1918, this time on the initiative of ecclesiastically-minded laymen, the Bishops declined to take fresh action in the matter.

[Further particulars with regard to this bit of history will be found in *The Faith of the Apostles' Creed* (Macmillan, 1918) Preface xxvi ff., in which an attempt was made to apply the method of religious construction, clause by clause, to the whole Creed, and in C. W. Emmet's *Conscience, Creeds, and Critics* (Macmillan, 1918), which contains also a valuable survey of earlier stages of the movement towards liberty of criticism within the Church of England.]

2. From the beginning the Church has taught the resurrection of all men. That resurrection it has consistently conceived as involving the reconstitution of their bodies as they had them in this world. God-fathers and godmothers in our Church, in bringing infants to baptism, still have to profess their belief in the resurrection of the flesh.

A few years ago a clergyman who knew that this view was the only one that was orthodox proclaimed his rejection of it, and a formal accusation of heresy was brought against him. The bishop of the diocese collected opinions from a few Professors of Divinity and then dismissed the charge, saying that the clergyman impugned took too limited a view of Catholic tradition:—his teaching on the subject did not constitute ground for establishing a charge of heresy against him.

Clergymen of the Church of England are thus absolved from a belief as to the mode of the resurrection which has been traditional in the Church all down the ages and can profess their faith in the Resurrection in the words of the Creed "the resurrection of the body", though they deny the literal meaning of the words.

[Full details of the teaching impugned, the opinions, and the bishop's decision are given in *The Doctrine of the Resurrection of the Body* issued by the Right Rev.

H. M. Burge, D.D., Lord Bishop of Oxford (A. R. Mowbray and Co., 1922) and *A Resurrection of Relics* by H. D. A. Major, B.D. (Basil Blackwell, Oxford, 1922).]

3. From seventy to fifty years ago the new theory of biological evolution was being fiercely contested by religious people. Now the truth of the main idea is assumed in all our schools and anything heard in our churches that is obviously not consistent with it is assumed to be somehow wrong. Our younger people think the parson ought to go to school again and seldom are they helped to discern the religious truth underlying the veneer of the old false science.

But recently, in an open letter to a brother bishop, the then Archbishop of Canterbury implied that he himself had long accepted the new views of creation and evolution, as far as he understood them.

It cannot, indeed, be said that the implications of the new knowledge are much in evidence in current theological teaching from the pulpit. It is not easy to re-interpret in evolutionist terms a system of doctrine founded on old ideas of creation and the Fall of Man, catastrophic changes and arbitrary interventions. But progress is being made, and I invite attention to the liberty which is now enjoyed in the Church of England, with high ecclesiastical authority for those who need it, to seek for and to offer in their presentation of Christian truth new interpretations on evolutionist lines.

Adaptation of oneself to a new environment is the only way of life in every department of human interest and activity. The instances I have given shew that the Church of England is still pursuing this way, able to comprehend within it different valuations of its order, different conceptions of our common Christian religion, and different methods of seeking to commend it. It has held its different schools of thought together because no one of them can justly aver that the official statements of the Church, or its rubrics, or its practice admit of only their own interpretation. Individual liberty to adventure within the limits of public order in every sphere of thought and action has been the secret of the stability and progress of the English people. The same spirit is alive in the Church of England.

[Of special value in this connexion are the later writings of Dr J. M. Wilson†, especially the chapter "The religious effect of the idea of Evolution" in *Evolution in the light of modern knowledge* (Blackie and Son, 1925), *Christianity in the light of the idea of Evolution* (*Guardian* Occasional Papers No. 3, April 1926), and *The Theological Outlook* (The D Society Pamphlets No. 1, 1924, Bowes and Bowes, Cambridge); *Christian Doctrine and the Idea of Evolution* by J. S. Boys Smith (The D Society Pamphlets No. 3, 1930); and the first section of the Report of the Lambeth Conference of 1930 on The Christian Doctrine of God.]

4. The only authoritative expression of the mind of the Church of England with regard to the constitution of the Church is given in the Articles of Religion and the Preface to the Ordinal.

The Articles are arranged in groups. There is in one group definition of the Church and of ministry in the Church, which was intended to be of general or universal application, and there is another group of articles of which the application is special to the Church of England.

That is to say, a distinction is drawn between the essential notes of a Church (Articles XIX, XXIII and XXV) and the particular constitution of the Church of England (Article XXXVI).

The visible Church of Christ is to be seen wherever there is a congregation of faithful men, in which the pure Word of God is preached and the Sacraments are duly ministered according to Christ's ordinance in all those things that of necessity are requisite to the same.

And there is declared to be due ministry wherever the organization of the congregation thus described includes provision for a succession of ministers appointed by men who have had public authority given to them in the congregation to choose and call others to this work—the Latin shewing, as the English does not, that the appointing authority are themselves ministers.

It is as part of the Church of England's own constitution that archbishops and bishops and priests and deacons are specified (Article xxxvi), not as a necessary note of the constitution of the visible Church of Christ, and the Preface to the Ordinal (to which the article refers) avoids any claim that the three orders of ministry are of the *esse* of the Church. This Preface asserts (what is not literally true) that "from the Apostles' time there have been these Orders of Ministers in Christ's Church: Bishops, Priests, and Deacons", and it expresses the intention "that these Orders may be continued, and reverently used and esteemed, in the Church of England". That is the position. The Church of England uses and esteems episcopacy: it is not committed to the theory that it is essential to the constitution of the Church.

It may be true that a wider view of the Church than had been current was forced upon the Church of England by the circumstances of the Reformation which proceeded on the principle of the recognition of national churches and their rights. But the fact remains that it did not assert that episcopacy was among the essentials of the Church, and ever since variant views on the subject have been held in the Church of England. Unity within the Church of England does not mean being of one mind as to whether bishops are of the *esse* or of the *bene esse* of the Church or whether in point of order they are among the "things indifferent". Hooker's position on this particular point is as tenable in the Church of England to-day as it was in the sixteenth century. These facts are known to all honest students of its history, but they need to be recalled and reaffirmed.

[They are apparently not known to the writer of the leading article in *The Times* of Saturday, June 23, 1934, which might have received a Roman *imprimatur* as regards this point. He reproves the authors of a statement on "Church Unity" published in *The Times* the day before for saying that episcopacy is not among the essentials of the Church, because that statement "will give offence to a very large number of people who, no less than themselves, are members of the Church of England".

Hooker is a strong champion of the "regiment" of bishops as coming down from the Apostles and exceedingly beneficial in the Church, and he argues that the Scriptures support this form of government rather than any other. Yet he declares it reasonable and sensible to say "Bishops albeit they may avouch with conformity of truth that their authority hath thus descended even from the very apostles themselves, yet the absolute and everlasting continuance of it they cannot say that any commandment of the Lord doth enjoin; and therefore must acknowledge that the Church hath power by universal consent upon urgent cause to take it away, if thereunto she be constrained through the proud, tyrannical, and unreformable dealings of her bishops, whose regiment she hath thus long delighted in, because she hath found it good and requisite to be so governed" (*Laws of Ecclesiastical Polity* VII v 8).

That statement is not altogether free from ambiguity, but earlier in his argument Hooker has laid down the principle that the necessity of polity and regiment in all churches may be held, without holding any one certain form to be necessary for them all. This shews what his intention was. And he goes on to mention the case of the foreign reformed churches which had abandoned the episcopal form. He declines to attempt to determine whether in any particular case there was justification or not. He is content to lay down the principle that there might be. There could be a Church without bishops.]

www.ingramcontent.com/pod-product-compliance
Ingram Content Group UK Ltd.
Pitfield, Milton Keynes, MK11 3LW, UK
UKHW042149280225
455719UK00001B/218

9 781107 505759